"9Marks, as a ministry, has taken basic biblical teaching about the church and put it into the hands of pastors. I am unaware of any other tool that so thoroughly and practically helps Christians understand God's plan for the local church. I can't wait to use these studies in my own congregation."

**Jeramie Rinne,** Senior Pastor, Sanibel Community Church, Fort Meyers, Florida

"9Marks has done local church pastors an incredible service by writing these study guides. Clear, biblical, and practical, they introduce the biblical basis for a healthy church. But more importantly, they challenge and equip church members to be part of the process of improving their own church's health. The studies work for individual, small group, and larger group settings. I have used them for the last year at my own church and appreciate how easy they are to adapt to my own setting. I don't know of anything else like them. Highly recommended!"

**Michael Lawrence,** Senior Pastor, Hinson Baptist Church, Portland, Oregon; author, *Biblical Theology in the Life of the Church*

"This is a Bible study that is actually rooted in the Bible and involves actual study. In the 9Marks Healthy Church Study Guides series a new standard has been set for personal theological discovery and corresponding personal application. Rich exposition, compelling questions, and clear syntheses combine to give a guided tour of ecclesiology—the theology of the church. I know of no better curriculum for generating understanding of and involvement in the church than this. It will be a welcome resource in our church for years to come."

**Rick Holland,** Senior Pastor, Mission Road Bible Church, Prairie Village, Kansas

"In America today we have the largest churches in the history of our nation, but the least amount of impact for Christ's kingdom. Slick marketing and finely polished vision statements are a foundation of sand. The 9Marks Healthy Church Study Guides series is a refreshing departure from church-growth materials toward an in-depth study of God's word that will equip God's people with his vision for his church. These study guides will lead local congregations to abandon secular methodologies for church growth and instead rely on Christ's principles for developing healthy, God-honoring assemblies."

**Carl J. Broggi,** Senior Pastor, Community Bible Church, Beaufort, South Carolina; President, Search the Scriptures Radio Ministry

"Anyone who loves Jesus will love what Jesus loves. The Bible clearly teaches that Jesus loves the church. He knows about and cares for individual churches and wants them to be spiritually healthy and vibrant. Not only has Jesus laid down his life for the church but he has also given many instructions in his word regarding how churches are to live and function in the world. This series of Bible studies by 9Marks shows how Scripture teaches these things. Any Christian who works through this curriculum, preferably with other believers, will be helped to see in fresh ways the wisdom, love, and power of God in establishing the church on earth. These studies are biblical, practical, and accessible. I highly recommend this curriculum as a useful tool that will help any church embrace its calling to display the glory of God to a watching world."

**Thomas Ascol,** Executive Director, Founders Ministries; Pastor, Grace Baptist Church, Cape Coral, Florida

T0334869

**9MARKS HEALTHY CHURCH STUDY GUIDES**

# SENDING AND GOING TOGETHER: MISSIONS

Alex Duke
Mark Dever, General Editor
Jonathan Leeman, Managing Editor

HEALTHY CHURCH STUDY GUIDES

**:: CROSSWAY®**

WHEATON, ILLINOIS

*Sending and Going Together: Missions*

© 2024 by 9Marks

Published by Crossway
       1300 Crescent Street
       Wheaton, Illinois 60187

Cover design: Dual Identity

First printing 2024

Trade paperback ISBN: 978-1-4335-8823-5
ePub ISBN: 978-1-4335-8826-6

Crossway is a publishing ministry of Good News Publishers.

| CH | | | 32 | 31 | 30 | 29 | 28 | 27 | 26 | 25 | 24 |
|----|----|----|----|----|----|----|----|----|----|----|----|
| 14 | 13 | 12 | 11 | 10 | 9 | 8 | 7 | 6 | 5 | 4 | 3 | 2 | 1 |

# CONTENTS

# INTRODUCTION

What does the local church mean to you?

Maybe you love your church. You love the people. You love the preaching and the singing. You can't wait to show up on Sunday, and you cherish fellowship with other church members throughout the week.

Then again, maybe your church is just a place you show up to a couple times a month. You sneak in late, duck out early.

We at 9Marks are convinced that the local church is where God means to display his glory to the nations. And we want to help you catch this vision, together with your whole church.

The *9Marks Healthy Church Study Guides* are a series of six- or seven-week studies on each of the "nine marks of a healthy church" plus one introductory study. These marks are the core convictions of our ministry. To provide a quick introduction and biblical defense of this particular mark, missions, we've included a condensed chapter from the new edition of Mark Dever's book *Nine Marks of a Healthy Church*. We don't claim that these marks are the only important things about the church. But we do believe that they are biblical and therefore helpful for churches.

So, in these studies, we're going to work through the biblical foundations and practical application of each mark. The twelve studies are:

- *Built upon the Rock: The Church* (the introductory series)
- *Hearing God's Word: Expositional Preaching*
- *The Whole Truth About God: Biblical Theology*
- *God's Good News: The Gospel*
- *Reaching the Lost: Evangelism*
- *Real Change: Conversion*
- *Committing to One Another: Church Membership*

- *Guarding One Another: Church Discipline*
- *Growing One Another: Discipleship in the Church*
- *Leading One Another: Church Leadership*
- *Talking to God: Prayer*
- *Sending and Going Together: Missions*

Each session of these studies takes a close look at one or more passages of Scripture and considers how to apply it to the life of your congregation. We hope they are equally appropriate for Sunday schools, small groups, and other contexts where a group of two to two hundred people can gather to discuss God's word.

These studies are mainly driven by observation, interpretation, and application questions, so get ready to speak up! We also hope that these studies provide opportunities for people to reflect together on their experiences in the church, whatever those experiences may be.

The study you are now holding is called *Sending and Going Together*. It focuses on God's global purposes from Genesis to Revelation. Reflecting on the book of Acts, this study guide also addresses practical questions like, Who sends missionaries? What do they actually do? What kind of missions work should churches support? The goal of this study is to encourage local churches to obey the Great Commission with wisdom, prudence, and patience, pursuing faithfulness above all else and ultimately leaving the fruitfulness to the Lord.

Are you ready?

# WHAT SHOULD CHURCHES BELIEVE ABOUT MISSIONS?

BY MARK DEVER

*(Adapted from "Mark Nine" in* Nine Marks of a Healthy Church*)*

*Missions* is not a word we find in the Bible, but it is a biblical idea. Missions is taking the gospel across boundaries—especially the boundary of language. While evangelism is telling the gospel, sometimes to people who don't know it, *missions* is evangelism in a place and among a whole people where it's largely unknown. This mission is nothing less than "to transform the nature of humanity."[1] To transform in what way? To bring us into a reconciled relationship with God, our good Creator and Judge.

This is the basic storyline of the whole Bible. In the beginning, the scope of the Bible is cosmic. It is worldwide. God creates a world that he calls good, mankind falls, and God promises redemption. Then the story seems to restart on a very small scale. God calls one man from modern-day Iraq, Abram. In Genesis 12 God tells him that through him all the families of the earth would be blessed. So the trajectory is set for the Old Testament—God would bless Israel, the nation descended from Abram, as a precursor and as a means to bless the whole world. God's role in the world is shown in his decisive defeat of the mighty Egyptian Empire as he frees his people Israel from slavery.

And yet, as the Lord said through the prophet Isaiah to his special servant in Isaiah 49:6,

> It is too light a thing that you should be my servant
> to raise up the tribes of Jacob

---

[1] Rosaria Butterfield, *Openness Unhindered* (Pittsburgh, PA: Crown & Covenant, 2015), 18.

and to bring back the preserved of Israel;
I will make you as a light for the nations,
     that my salvation may reach the end of the earth.

So the servant comes: Jesus Christ is crucified and rises again. And the Son of God teaches his disciples, "All authority in heaven and on earth has been given to me. Go therefore and make disciples of all nations, baptizing them in the name of the Father and of the Son and of the Holy Spirit, teaching them to observe all that I have commanded you. And behold, I am with you always, to the end of the age" (Matt. 28:18–20). Jesus was saying, "As much as it takes and as long as it takes, I am with you to the end!" We see the disciples scattering in the book of Acts and the gospel going throughout the Mediterranean world and beyond, fulfilling Jesus's command. And we see its final fulfillment in the book of Revelation, which is filled with scenes like this:

> After this I looked, and behold, a great multitude that no one could number, from every nation, from all tribes and peoples and languages, standing before the throne and before the Lamb, clothed in white robes with palm branches in their hands, and crying out with a loud voice, "Salvation belongs to our God who sits on the throne, and to the Lamb!" (Rev. 7:9–10)

The basic story of the Bible was never merely ethnic and local or national and parochial—it was always as wide as the creation and the Creator's claims.

This is not the invention of some later missiologist. This is the basic idea of the Bible. Therefore, we must be especially clear about the gospel, the good news, that is at the heart of it all. This good news about Jesus Christ is so important that Paul calls for the damnation of any who would change the basic message of the gospel (see Gal. 1:8). This message is the means by which God will reconcile the world to himself, and so bring redemption to all who will trust in Christ.

The gospel of Jesus Christ is the only means of our being converted from spiritual death to spiritual life, from being condemned to being saved. This is how the apostle Paul understood his whole ministry. Paul recounted the risen Christ's words to him at his conversion on the road to Damascus:

> I have appeared to you for this purpose, to appoint you as a servant and witness to the things in which you have seen me and to those in which I will appear to you, delivering you from your people and from the Gentiles—to whom I am sending you to open their eyes, so that they may turn from darkness to light and from the power of Satan to God, that they may receive forgiveness of sins and a place among those who are sanctified by faith in me. (Acts 26:16–18)

This good news is what has led to our own conversions! And it is what we share with others in our evangelism.

This is the heart of everything we do. The nature of truly believing includes repenting of our sins, so there is in true Christianity a quality of self-denial. It's not the added optional extra mature thing to do—"if you feel really guilty, you can start living radically." No, you're not a Christian if you don't take up your cross. Repentance and faith are part of that basic gospel message as we pursue holiness, and as we love God and others. And it is in this combination of self-sacrifice and love of God and others that we find the seed of missions in our churches. If that seed of understanding the gospel is missing, then all the missions programs in the world won't do anything for us. Missions begins with our understanding of the gospel and conversion.

You could say that missions begins at home, with a concern for the conversion of your family. Teach, befriend, evangelize, and disciple your children. Have a concern for your friends; friends share the gospel with friends. What does it mean for you to be prepared to share the gospel at work with someone this week?

Establishing an evangelistic Bible study at your workplace may not be all that different from evangelizing in Singapore or Moscow. Evangelism requires the same basic components, no matter what the context may be. So don't wait to start evangelizing. Why not find a Muslim friend in your neighborhood and offer to read through the Koran with him if he'll read through the Bible with you? As you share the good news with real people, you prepare yourself to do that in any place God may call you.

As we grow in understanding the Bible's big picture, discipling Christians naturally becomes more important to us. So at Capitol Hill Baptist Church, we work for a culture of evangelism and discipling. This culture is the foundation of a culture of missions. Do not underestimate how you handicap missions in a church by making evangelism seem optional in the Christian life. Baked into our basic discipling of each other in Scripture and holiness should be a concern for evangelism and missions. How we as individuals spend our money is part of our church missions program. How we spend our time is too. Are you modeling that well? Are you being obedient in sharing the gospel? Are you modeling praying and giving, particularly for the gospel to go out to all the nations? That's how we participate in the big story of the Bible.

In coming to Christ, God moves us from being self-focused to God-focused. That causes us to notice others as spiritual beings, to think of the future of our children and youth, to reach out in evangelism to others who don't know the Lord yet, and then, ultimately, to go into the whole world, teaching those who have never heard the good news. So missions isn't something occasional and optional; it is an essential extension of what God has always been about in this world, to bring glory to himself through us. Healthy churches are marked by a biblical understanding and practice of missions. But if these gospel seeds are in place in our churches, what will that look like in practice?

# WEEK 1
# IS MISSIONS JUST A
# NEW TESTAMENT THING?

## GETTING STARTED

*1. What Old Testament passages come to mind when you think about God's plan for the nations?*

*2. What is the role of Israel in God's plan for the nations? How does this connect to the church?*

When most Christians think about missions in the Bible, they think about the Great Commission. That's a vital, important passage—and we'll get to it. But God's plan for his people to make his name known among the nations doesn't start in the New Testament. In fact, it can be found in the earliest pages of Scripture.

Though Scripture devotes the bulk of its pages to the story of the nation of Israel, its primary burden is to call all people everywhere to worship the Lord—after all, the God of the Bible is the Lord of the universe, just as Jesus Christ is the Savior of the world.

## MAIN IDEA

The burden to take God's message of salvation to the nations is seen all throughout Scripture, not just the New Testament.

## DIGGING IN

Consider God's promise to Abraham. We often think of this as the establishment of Israel, and that's true. But it doesn't tell the whole story. Pay attention to how the promise ends:

> Go from your country and your kindred and your father's house to the land that I will show you. And I will make of you a great nation,

and I will bless you and make your name great, so that you will be a blessing. I will bless those who bless you, and him who dishonors you I will curse, and in you all the families of the earth shall be blessed. (Gen. 12:1–3)

Through Abraham, God intends to create a people who will make his name great *among the nations* through their faithful obedience. He blesses Abraham and his kindred so that they might be a blessing. He promises to make Abraham's name great so long as Abraham commits to making God's name great. The rest of Scripture unfolds according to the dividing line introduced here: Do you trust the Lord's plan to do this and, in the process, receive his blessings? Or do you trust in your own power and, in the process, curse the Lord and eventually curse yourself?

Of course, Israel fails—miserably. In fact, they eventually fail so spectacularly that they seem to lose their special status as God's treasured people and end up in exile, under the thumb of blasphemous enemies.

During this time in Israel's history, the Lord raises up prophets to communicate God's word to God's people. Unsurprisingly, their message consists of a lot of judgment. That's the dominant theme. And yet, through it all, God not only reiterates his promise of blessing to his people but also paints a picture of a future time when the blessings of Israel would extend to the whole world.

This drumbeat of God's heart for the nations begins in Genesis. Though it gets muffled by sin quite quickly, there are many places before the Gospels where it is amplified. The goal of this introductory study will be to acquaint you with a few of those places in the book of Isaiah. If you're not familiar with Isaiah, then consider consulting the *ESV Study Bible* notes on the book.

*1. There are lots of places in Scripture that talk about God's plan for the nations. Let's visit a surprising one: Isaiah 19. Read this passage and summarize how it shows God's heart for the nations.*

*2. What stands out to you from Isaiah 19?*

*3. Isaiah 42 introduces a new character in the prophecy to God's people: the "servant of the LORD" (v. 19). What does Isaiah 42:1–10 say about him and what he will do? What does his arrival signal? (Note: the "you" in 42:6–9 shows Yahweh speaking to his servant, and the "servant" in 42:19–25 is referring to Israel as a sinful nation.)*

*4. How does Isaiah 42 portray the connection between the global mission of God and the glory of God?*

*5. Isaiah 49 picks up where Isaiah 42 left off and tells us more about this servant. What do we learn in this passage?*

*6. After the surprising description of what this servant will endure (Isa. 53), Isaiah then unfolds at length God's glorious plan and invites the whole world to participate. Read Isaiah 54–56 and jot down anything that stands out to you.*

*7. How does the book of Isaiah end? (Read Isaiah 66.)*

*8. In light of this brief overview of Isaiah, how would you try to explain to someone that God's burden for the nations is clear all throughout Scripture? What does all this have to do with Jesus and the mission of his new people, the church? Do any New Testament uses of Isaiah help clarify this question? (See, for example, Romans 2:24; 15:12; Luke 2:32.)*

# WEEK 2
# WHAT IS A CHURCH AND
# WHAT IS ITS MISSION?

## GETTING STARTED

*1. If someone asked you why the local church exists, how would you respond?*

*2. What common things pass as missions work that might not actually qualify?*

We need to know what a thing *is* before we know what it's supposed to *do*. For example, most men who walk into an Ulta Beauty will be surrounded by foreign objects with little discernible purpose. The same goes for many women who walk into a Bass Pro Shop. If you don't know what a thing is, you're probably not going to know what it's supposed to do. Is that for eyelashes or eyebrows? Is that for hunting or fishing?

So, what is a church? Hopefully you've gone through other studies in this series that help answer that question. If not, that's okay. Here's an abbreviated answer: a church is a group of baptized Christians who have covenanted with one another under the leadership of the Lord Jesus. So a church isn't a building or a group of leaders or a religious service. A church is a people.

"Okay," you say, "but what are these people supposed to *do?*" Do these baptized, covenanted-together Christians have a unique job to do?

The answer, of course, is yes. The church does have a unique job, that is, a job that can't be accomplished by individual Christians, faith-based non-profits, or parachurch ministries. That job is summarized by the Great Commission.

## MAIN IDEA

The Great Commission is given to the church, and it shapes the church's mission.

## DIGGING IN

Before we get to the Great Commission, let's rewind a bit to the first time the word "church" shows up in the Bible. Sam Emadi explains this well: "In Matthew 16, Jesus asks the apostles who they think he is. Peter pipes up first: 'You are the Christ, the Son of the living God' (Matt. 16:16). Jesus's reply to Peter is a stunning statement not just about Peter but about all those who imitate Peter's faith."[2] The next verses read,

> And Jesus answered him, "Blessed are you, Simon Bar-Jonah! For flesh and blood has not revealed this to you, but my Father who is in heaven. And I tell you, you are Peter, and on this rock I will build my church, and the gates of hell shall not prevail against it. I will give you the keys of the kingdom of heaven, and whatever you bind on earth shall be bound in heaven, and whatever you loose on earth shall be loosed in heaven."

Emadi further explains that

> Jesus is going to build his church on Peter—the confessor and his confession. But more than that, Jesus is going to give Peter and the other apostles the "keys of the kingdom of heaven," such that they, like Jesus, declare confessions of faith as from heaven. Perhaps even more remarkable, however, is that Jesus gives this same authority ("the keys of the kingdom of heaven") not just to the apostles, but to local churches of ordinary men and women who believe in Jesus.[3]

Matthew 18:15–20 tells us,

> If your brother sins against you, go and tell him his fault, between you and him alone. If he listens to you, you have gained your

---

[2] Sam Emadi, *Who's In Charge at Church?* (Wheaton, IL: Crossway, 2022), 18.
[3] Sam Emadi, "Be Like Batman: Guard the Gospel," 9Marks, March 30, 2021, https://www.9marks .org/.

brother. But if he does not listen, take one or two others along with you, that every charge may be established by the evidence of two or three witnesses. If he refuses to listen to them, tell it to the church. And if he refuses to listen even to the church, let him be to you as a Gentile and a tax collector. Truly, I say to you, whatever you bind on earth shall be bound in heaven, and whatever you loose on earth shall be loosed in heaven. Again I say to you, if two of you agree on earth about anything they ask, it will be done for them by my Father in heaven. For where two or three are gathered in my name, there am I among them.

All of this is vital background for the Great Commission. It helps the reader understand that the church—that is, those who agree with Peter's confession; those who gather in the name of Jesus—are also the ones who Jesus sends out to make disciples and baptize in his name, spurred on by his ever-present authority. With this background in mind, read the Great Commission:

Now the eleven disciples went to Galilee, to the mountain to which Jesus had directed them. And when they saw him they worshiped him, but some doubted. And Jesus came and said to them, "All authority in heaven and on earth has been given to me. Go therefore and make disciples of all nations, baptizing them in the name of the Father and of the Son and of the Holy Spirit, teaching them to observe all that I have commanded you. And behold, I am with you always, to the end of the age." (Matt. 28:16–20)

Overall, these passages in Matthew's Gospel don't exhaust everything we need to know about the church and its mission. But they do describe its essence, its foundation, its leading edge. All of this deserves our prayerful reflection.

*1. What stands out to you about these three passages? How are they connected?*

*2. When you read Jesus's words, "The gates of hell shall not prevail against it" (Matt. 16:18), what image comes to your mind? Read the passage carefully and explain how it depicts the church on the offense, not the church in a defensive posture, guarding against threats.*

*3. What are the keys of the kingdom for? How do Matthew 16 and 18 help you answer that question?*

*4. Who is the Great Commission given to?*

*5. How does Matthew 28:20 lead us to church planting and not just disciple making as the goal of the Great Commission?*

*6. From these passages in Matthew, explain how the church has a unique mission that is controlled by a unique confidence.*

*7. In light of these passages, what kinds of things could be properly described as "fulfilling" or "obeying" the Great Commission? What things, while still good, would not qualify as fulfilling or obeying the Great Commission?*

*8. Why does this work require patience?*

# WEEK 3
# WHAT DO MISSIONARIES DO?

## GETTING STARTED

*1. Describe the day-to-day life of a missionary.*

*2. Is every Christian a missionary? Why or why not?*

When we hear the word "missionaries," some of us picture airplanes, jungles, and a few grizzled, mature Christians who spend half their time preaching and the other half of their time praying. Other Christians picture orphanages full of smiling children and medical professionals who donate their time and expertise. Still others picture a small group of converts huddling in their homes, singing in whispers so they don't get caught by lurking authorities.

Depending on which missionaries you know, those pictures are more or less accurate. Though these depictions differ in a lot of ways, one assumption persists: whatever missionaries do, it doesn't really look like my normal Christian life.

That's true—sort of. Missionaries aren't normal; every Christian isn't a missionary. And yet, many missionaries' lives look a lot like our everyday lives. They're ordinarily faithful in often extraordinary places.

Though the word "missions" doesn't appear in the Bible, it's a biblical idea with a simple definition: taking the gospel across boundaries, especially linguistic boundaries and usually geographic ones. That's what missionaries do. They take the gospel to people who need it and to people who aren't like them. But they do so with a goal in mind. They don't just want to see individual conversions— they want to see groups of new converts gather into churches. That brings us to the main idea of this third study.

## SENDING AND GOING TOGETHER

### MAIN IDEA

The task of the missionary is to make disciples, which means to preach the gospel and cultivate healthy churches in places where there are few healthy churches.

### DIGGING IN

Paul and Barnabas were missionaries. In Acts 13, the church at Antioch of Syria sends them out. Then the next chapter is full of drama: they face intense persecution and Paul is stoned to the point of near death. And yet, as obstacles arise, they never stop preaching the word.

If we were to chart their journey, it wouldn't look like a perfect circle. It might look more like a toddler's drawings. They go to one place, then another, and then out of the way to another place. Then they circle back to where they were previously. Here's how all that movement gets summed up, with a few editorial notes added in brackets:

> But Jews came [to Lystra] from Antioch and Iconium, and having persuaded the crowds, they stoned Paul and dragged him out of the city, supposing that he was dead. But when the disciples gathered about him, he rose up and entered the city, and on the next day he went on with Barnabas to Derbe. When they had preached the gospel to that city [Derbe] and had made many disciples, they returned to Lystra [where Paul just got stoned!] and to Iconium [where they'd already been in 14:1–6] and to Antioch [of Pisidia, where they'd already been in 13:13–43], strengthening the souls of the disciples, encouraging them to continue in the faith, and saying that through many tribulations we must enter the kingdom of God. And when they had appointed elders for them in every church, with prayer and fasting they committed them to the Lord in whom they had believed. Then they passed through Pisidia and came to Pamphylia [a region they had already been to in 13:13]. And when they had spoken the word in Perga [a city in the region of Pamphylia], they went down to Attalia, and from there they sailed to Antioch [of Syria, not Pisidia!], where they had been commended to the grace of God for the work that they had fulfilled. And when they arrived and gathered the church together, they declared all that God had done with them, and how he had opened

a door of faith to the Gentiles. And they remained no little time with the disciples. (Acts 14:19–28)

Paul and Barnabas were called to a work. That work included more than one thing. But what was the main thing, the primary thing, the thing that made sure they would take the long route and retrace their steps and even return to cities that had persecuted them, pushed them out, and tried to murder them? It was preaching the gospel and making many disciples; it was encouraging those disciples to endure; it was establishing those new believers in healthy churches led by godly elders and entrusting them to the Lord through prayer and fasting.

That's why Paul and Barnabas return to Antioch of Syria to declare "all that God had done with them." They then stay there with those disciples for "no little time."

Put simply, Matthew 28:16–20 is the Great Commission exhorted and Acts 13–14 is the Great Commission obeyed. The Great Commission is about the establishing and strengthening of healthy, local churches. It's a patient, necessary work. This means that missionaries are primarily committed to certain tasks.

*1. What is a missionary's job? How is that job the same as every Christian's? How is it different?*

*2. What connections do you see between Acts 13–14 and Matthew 28:16–20?*

*3. Chart out on your own each leg of this journey, including where Paul and Barnabas went and what they did when they got there.*

*4. Why do you think they would appoint leaders in the churches? Why was that such an important task?*

*5. "Missions is more than evangelism." What do you think about this statement?*

*6. In light of these passages, what kinds of things could be properly described as fulfilling or obeying the Great Commission? What things, while still good, would not qualify as fulfilling or obeying the Great Commission? Have your answers to these questions changed after two weeks in this study?*

*7. Why does this work require patience? Has your answer to this question changed after two weeks in this study?*

# WEEK 4
# WHERE DO MISSIONARIES COME FROM?

### GETTING STARTED

*1. What is the difference between a missionary's relationship with their sending church and their relationship with their sending organization?*

*2. Who is responsible for identifying and raising up missionaries?*

So far, we've seen that God's burden for the nations is clear from the first pages of Scripture. We've also seen how the Great Commission shapes the church's mission and that the primary job of missionaries is to preach the gospel and patiently plant healthy churches. We've seen this modeled clearly through Paul and Barnabas in Acts 13 and 14.

But let's back up a bit. How did Paul and Barnabas get there? We've said the church at Antioch "sent them off" (Acts 13:3). But what does that mean, and does it have any bearing on missionaries today?

### MAIN IDEA

Missionaries are tested, affirmed, and sent out by local churches—not by missions agencies and certainly not by themselves or other individuals.

### DIGGING IN

Who is responsible for identifying, training, and sending out missionaries? And once missionaries arrive on the field, who is responsible for them? Anyone at all? Or are they just lone rangers?

To address these questions, let's return to Acts 13. Here's how Luke describes the departure of Barnabas and Paul (called "Saul" here):

> Now there were in the church at Antioch prophets and teachers, Barnabas, Simeon who was called Niger, Lucius of Cyrene, Manaen a lifelong friend of Herod the tetrarch, and Saul. While they were worshiping the Lord and fasting, the Holy Spirit said, "Set apart for me Barnabas and Saul for the work to which I have called them." Then after fasting and praying they laid their hands on them and sent them off. (Acts 13:1–3)

The church at Antioch is our template for sending missionaries; it shows us what this endeavor should look like. Let's remember exactly how we got here. Barnabas had been sent by the Jerusalem church to Antioch to hear a report of the Lord's work outside Jesus's hometown (Acts 11:19–22). Barnabas shows up there and "sees" God's grace at work (Acts 15:36). This makes him glad, and so he encourages the church to remain steadfast in the faith.

What does he do next? He goes to Paul's hometown and recruits him to join the effort in Antioch. Luke summarizes their next step: "For a whole year they met with the church and taught a great many people. And in Antioch the disciples were first called Christians" (Acts 11:26). By now, both Paul and Barnabas are a part of the church in Antioch, even as they travel back to Jerusalem at the behest of the elders to give them financial relief from a coming drought (Acts 11:27–30).

Why all this backstory? Well, because when we read Acts 13:1–3, it might sound like no big deal that this church in Antioch sends out Paul and Barnabas. But when we remember their shared history, we remember that by sending out these two men, this church sent out their best. Simeon, Lucius, and Manaen knew who they were losing by sending out these men, but they also knew what they were gaining. They knew that they had benefited from Barnabas because of the generosity of the church in Jerusalem.

Mack Stiles rightly says that "we desperately need a rigorous application of Acts 13 today. It isn't about churches being willing to sign off on someone" who's sincere or sending a check and hearing an annual update.[4] Rather, "it's about churches sending out biblically qualified, carefully examined partners for the work."[5] When a church sends out a missionary, it should sting.

1. *Read through Acts 11:19–30. What stands out to you?*

2. *In light of what you've read in Acts, what does a church need to know about someone in order to send them out as a missionary?*

3. *In what ways is the calling of Paul and Barnabas unique?*

4. *In what ways is the calling of Paul and Barnabas paradigmatic?*

5. *As we've already seen, in Acts 14:24–28 Paul and Barnabas return to Antioch and give a report about their missionary journey. What does this communicate about their continued relationship with the Antioch church?*

6. *What does your answer to the previous question teach you about the continued accountability that missionaries have to their sending churches? Practically speaking, what might that accountability look like?*

7. *The Bible doesn't have anything to say about missions agencies because they didn't exist yet. But in light of the principles put forward here, what role should agencies have in the missionary enterprise? What should they do and not do?*

---

[4] Mack Stiles, "Don't Go Until You're Sent," the Gospel Coalition, February 27, 2017, https://www.thegospelcoalition.org/.

[5] Stiles, "Don't Go Until You're Sent."

# WEEK 5
# WHAT KIND OF MISSIONS WORK SHOULD CHURCHES SUPPORT?

## GETTING STARTED

*1. Someone comes up to you and says, "It's not missions work if it's not done among unreached people." What do you say?*

*2. What kind of training do you think missionaries should receive?*

How did the gospel get from the lips of the apostles to your ears? Wouldn't it be fun to be able to see that centuries-long, complicated chain of events? Who shared the gospel with whom until it got to you?

The Great Commission has been the unbroken burden of Christians for nearly two millennia. Throughout these years, untold fortunes have been freely given in order to support a subset of Christians who desired to devote their entire lives to this endeavor. As we've seen, the bulk of that task has fallen on churches partnering together—whether from Antioch and Jerusalem in the first century or Atlanta and New Jersey in the twenty-first.

## MAIN IDEA

While missions is more than evangelizing and planting churches among the unreached, our obedience to the Great Commission must include those elements.

## DIGGING IN

One of the clearest examples of this comes near the end of Paul's letter to the Roman church. As it turns out, the book of Romans isn't just a majestic theological treatise. It's also, believe it or not, a missionary support letter. Here's what he writes:

> I myself am satisfied about you, my brothers, that you yourselves are full of goodness, filled with all knowledge and able to instruct one another. But on some points I have written to you very boldly by way of reminder, because of the grace given me by God to be a minister of Christ Jesus to the Gentiles in the priestly service of the gospel of God, so that the offering of the Gentiles may be acceptable, sanctified by the Holy Spirit. In Christ Jesus, then, I have reason to be proud of my work for God. For I will not venture to speak of anything except what Christ has accomplished through me to bring the Gentiles to obedience—by word and deed, by the power of signs and wonders, by the power of the Spirit of God—so that from Jerusalem and all the way around to Illyricum I have fulfilled the ministry of the gospel of Christ; and thus I make it my ambition to preach the gospel, not where Christ has already been named, lest I build on someone else's foundation, but as it is written,
>
> "Those who have never been told of him will see,
> and those who have never heard will understand."
>
> This is the reason why I have so often been hindered from coming to you. But now, since I no longer have any room for work in these regions, and since I have longed for many years to come to you, I hope to see you in passing as I go to Spain, and to be helped on my journey there by you, once I have enjoyed your company for a while. At present, however, I am going to Jerusalem bringing aid to the saints. For Macedonia and Achaia have been pleased to make some contribution for the poor among the saints at Jerusalem. For they were pleased to do it, and indeed they owe it to them. For if the Gentiles have come to share in their spiritual blessings, they ought also to be of service to them in material blessings. When therefore I have completed this and have delivered to them what has been collected, I will leave for Spain by way of you. I know that when I come to you I will come in the fullness of the blessing of Christ. (Rom. 15:14–29)

This is what the Great Commission's ever-expanding reach looks like in real time. Paul knew that Jesus had told them to make disciples of "all nations" (Matt 28:19). He knew that Jesus, just before he ascended into heaven, told his disciples that they were to be his witnesses not only in Jerusalem, Judea, and Samaria but to the very ends of the earth. To us, Spain doesn't sound like that exotic of a place. But for Paul, Spain was the ends of the earth as he knew it.

As we saw in Acts 13–14, the work of missions is the work of planting and strengthening healthy local churches led by qualified elders. As we see here in Romans 15, this work is animated by a desire to see the gospel—and therefore healthy local churches—spread to places that are in desperate need. So while missions isn't, strictly speaking, exclusively about work among the unreached, that work must be a part of a church's overall missions strategy.

*1. In what sense has Paul "fulfilled" his ministry in verse 19?*

*2. What is Paul's new ambition?*

*3. Where in the Old Testament does Paul find his motivation for his ambition?*

*4. Paul says that he "no longer ha[s] any room for work in these regions," which explains why he now has different ambitions (Rom. 15:23). What practical lessons might Paul's self-assessment have for our missions strategies today?*

*5. What is Paul's direct request of the Roman church in 15:24?*

*6. One of the things Paul asks for is "help" for his journey (Rom. 15:24). Why do you think he follows up that request with his story about the saints of Macedonia and Achaia helping the church in Jerusalem?*

*7. Why does Paul say the saints in Macedonia and Achaia "owe" (15:27) support to the saints in Jerusalem?*

*8. This passage is full of practical logistics. Paul is coordinating missions and relief work here with full confidence not only in the Lord but also in his brothers and sisters. What lessons for today can you draw from this?*

# WEEK 6
# WHAT KIND OF
# MISSIONARIES SHOULD
# CHURCHES SUPPORT?

## GETTING STARTED

*1. How can churches know what their supported workers are doing?*

*2. Who are missionaries accountable to once they're on the field?*

So far, we've talked about what kind of missions work churches should support. But what kind of *missionaries* should they support? When should a church refuse a missionary? These are important questions. Thankfully, Scripture offers some guidelines on how to answer them.

## MAIN IDEA

Scripture puts forward the criteria for the kind of missionaries we should support and the kind of missionaries we must avoid.

## DIGGING IN

A few passages help us to understand how churches should financially support prospective missionaries. One we've already mentioned; two others come from frequently overlooked books: 2 John and 3 John. Let's start with the message of 3 John, which is reminiscent of Paul's request in Romans 15.

John is writing to Gaius, probably an elder at a local church. Apparently, John had been visited by Christians from Gaius's church who told John about their pastor Gaius's faithful Christian life. Here's what he writes to encourage Gaius:

> Beloved, it is a faithful thing you do in all your efforts for these brothers, strangers as they are, who testified to your love before the church. You will do well to send them on their journey in a manner worthy of God. For they have gone out for the sake of the name, accepting nothing from the Gentiles. Therefore we ought to support people like these, that we may be fellow workers for the truth. (3 John 5–8)

Did you notice how John ends his comment with an argument? "Therefore," he says, we Christians should support "people like these," that is, those who have gone out for the sake of the gospel. Interestingly, that word "send" in 3 John 6 is the same word that Paul uses in Romans 15:24. There, it gets translated as "helped." In both cases, financial support is in view.

Now, let's look at a passage where John encourages the opposite response—not acceptance but refusal. He writes,

> And this is love, that we walk according to his commandments; this is the commandment, just as you have heard from the beginning, so that you should walk in it. For many deceivers have gone out into the world, those who do not confess the coming of Jesus Christ in the flesh. Such a one is the deceiver and the antichrist. Watch yourselves, so that you may not lose what we have worked for, but may win a full reward. Everyone who goes on ahead and does not abide in the teaching of Christ, does not have God. Whoever abides in the teaching has both the Father and the Son. If anyone comes to you and does not bring this teaching, do not receive him into your house or give him any greeting, for whoever greets him takes part in his wicked works. (2 John 6–11)

John repeats a common theme in his writings: Christians must hold fast to the truth that has been faithfully handed down to them. How do we know the difference between a Christian and a deceiver, between someone who trusts God and someone who doesn't? We know based on how they walk (v. 6), what they confess (v. 7), and what they teach (v. 9–10).

In 3 John, we see what to look for in missionaries worth supporting; in 2 John, we see what to look for in missionaries worth avoiding.

1. Read the whole book of 3 John (don't worry, it's short!). What stands out to you, particularly about missions?


2. John tells Gaius to send those brothers "in a manner worthy of God" (3 John 6). What do you think that looks like?


3. Why does John say these men deserve that kind of support (v. 7)?


4. What does "gone out for the sake of the name" mean (v. 7)? What does this teach us about who we should send with this kind of support? What kind of relationship should they have with their sending church?


5. Read the whole book of 2 John (don't worry, it's even shorter!). What stands out to you, particularly about missions?


6. According to 2 John, what are the criteria for determining whether someone is a deceptive, fake missionary or a genuine, real missionary?


7. How should we respond to fake missionaries? What happens if we refuse to respond to them in the way we should?


8. In light of your answers to the last two questions, how should churches determine the worthiness of both prospective missionaries and current missionaries? What processes need to exist on the front end? What processes might be useful for ongoing partnerships? Try to be as concrete as possible in your answers.


9. Apart from false teaching, what else might disqualify a missionary from church support?

# TEACHER'S NOTES FOR WEEK 1

## DIGGING IN

1. The context here is important: through Isaiah, the Lord is judging Judah for turning to Egypt—their former foe—for help when they were threatened by Assyria. So we begin the chapter expecting a harsh word against Egypt, and that's precisely what we get in 19:1–15. But then comes a shocking reversal. The rest of the oracle explains how God will eventually restore Egypt and all the nations, treating them like Judah. "In that day"— repeated six times—lets the reader know that this will happen in some undetermined but inevitable future. Note especially the promise in verses 19–22. There will be an altar that functions as a sign and a witness to the Egyptian people, and the Lord will send them a savior and a defender. Yes, even Egypt, the nation that balled up its fist in defiance against the Lord (Ex. 1–15) will one day be healed and shown mercy; they will be a "blessing in the midst of the earth" (v. 24). Of them, the Lord will say, "These are my people" (v. 25). Amazing!

2. Answers will vary.

3. This "servant" will be Spirit-indwelled and chosen by God to bring forth justice to the nations (vv. 1, 3, 4). The Lord speaks over this servant and says that he has called him to be "a light for the nations, to open the eyes that are blind" (vv. 6–7). This, the Lord says, is a new thing that he will do (v. 9) through his servant.

4. Focus on 42:8–12 here. These new declarations from the Lord make it clear that his name will be glorified throughout the world in ways never seen before. The *ESV Study Bible* explains,

> Both the triumph of Cyrus (41:2–4, 25–29) and the greater triumph of the servant glorify the true Lord of history and discredit idolatrous claims of human mastery. The God who has promised the world-transforming display of his glory (40:5) directs all events as he pleases to that final end. God must discredit all idols to receive his proper honor. He is not one of many; he is not superior among inferior gods; he is not even the best of all; he is the *only* God, and he will have his people know and rejoice in this truth. . . . God deliberately draws attention to the seemingly impossible predictions he is

making, citing his previous prophecies as evidence of his credibility (cf. 41:22). . . . [What we read in 42:10 is] unprecedented praise, such as has never been heard before, marking the greatness of the revelation of the servant in history.[6]

5. The servant of the Lord will not only restore Israel but also save the nations. Notice the escalation in 49:5–6. It's "too light a thing" to raise up the tribes of Jacob. Instead, this servant must also be a "light for the nations, that [God's] salvation may reach to the end of the earth." Again, amazing!

6. Answers will vary.

7. The *ESV Study Bible* summarizes this chapter as follows:

Though the worship of God is violated now, in the future falsehood will be judged, true worship will spread, and God will be honored forever. . . . God's glory is declared worldwide, and man's rebellion is punished forever. . . . The cosmos, which bore witness to Israel's sins in 1:2–3, is renewed as the environment for the endless worship of the new people of God, who represent all flesh. God will keep his every promise to the praise of his glorious grace.[7]

8. There are many potential answers to this question. In Luke 2:30–32, Jesus is identified as "a light for the Gentiles," which recalls Isaiah 49:5–6. Many New Testament passages about Jesus's death recall Isaiah 53 (Matt. 27:14, 46; John 1:10–11; 2 Cor. 5:21; 1 Pet. 2:23–25). Perhaps the clearest is Acts 8:33–35, which explicitly connects Jesus to the servant in Isaiah. For a connection to the broader message of the book of Isaiah, consider Luke 4:16–22. Jesus reads a chunk of Isaiah (61:1–2; 58:6) and then applies everything he reads to himself. He *is* the Spirit-filled Messiah of Isaiah, and he's come to do everything the Lord said he would do. Further, Jesus's ministry shows us the surprising fact that the suffering servant of Isaiah 53 is the same person as the victorious servant of Isaiah 49.

---

[6] Raymond C. Ortlund Jr., study notes for Isaiah in *ESV Study Bible* (Wheaton, IL: Crossway, 2008), 1316.
[7] Ortlund, study notes for Isaiah, 1360, 1362.

# TEACHER'S NOTES FOR WEEK 2

## DIGGING IN

1. Answers will vary. Matthew 16, 18, and 28 describe the essential confession of the church, the delegated authority of the church, and the necessary task of the church.

2. Contrary to popular belief, "The gates of hell shall not prevail against it" (Matt. 16:18) isn't a promise that the church will endure against Satan and sin even as they assault us from every side. Instead, this is a promise that Christians can confidently storm the gates of hell because those gates cannot stand up against the proclamation of the gospel. In other words, Jesus wins, so let's get to work!

3. The keys of the kingdom refer to the authority given to the church to make heaven's judgments here on earth. They are given to all who gather in Jesus's name (18:20), that is, those who agree with Peter's profession of faith about Jesus from Matthew 16.

4. The Great Commission is given first to the remaining disciples but its concluding promise—"I will be with you until the end of the age" (Matt. 28:20)—makes it clear that this commission is for all believers until Jesus comes back. It endures until he returns. So we can rightly say that the Great Commission is given to the church. Jesus has all authority, and he's given some of that authority to his church, to those who gather in his name. These churches have a job to do: storm the gates of hell with the gospel, baptize those who believe the gospel, and then teach all that Jesus commanded to those new disciples. On and on the cycle goes until Jesus comes back, when our faith becomes sight and his presence with us is fully realized.

5. In short, "teaching them to obey all that I have commanded" (Matt. 28:20) is a long process. So the goal of the Great Commission isn't simply to lead a group of people to make a profession of Christ. Rather, the goal is to create healthy churches full of disciples who are living as Jesus taught his church to live.

6. No other institution except the local church can bank on the promise that "the gates of hell will not prevail against" it (Matt. 28:20). This means the church has a unique confidence. Similarly, no other institution except the local church has been told to go into the world and make disciples by

baptizing them and then teaching them to obey everything Jesus commanded. This means the church has a unique mission. Notice that the keys of the kingdom are not given to any individual believer but to those who gather in Jesus's name. Peter didn't have the keys and then hand them down to his successor. Rather, the keys of the kingdom are freely given to all those groups of believers called "churches" who follow in Peter's footsteps by looking at Jesus and saying, "You are the Christ, the Son of the Living God!" (Matt. 16:16).

7. Fulfilling the Great Commission includes evangelism, church planting, disciple making, and missions among unreached people groups. Activities that do not directly fulfill the Great Commission but are still worthwhile include, for example, fighting global famine and human trafficking, digging wells for clean water, and picketing against abortion. The list is long. All of these tasks are noble and good, and Christians should pursue them freely and boldly! But they should not be collapsed into the mission of the church.

8. Because Jesus didn't tell us when he's coming back, we shouldn't try to reverse engineer circumstances that we think will hasten his return. Furthermore, the process of teaching someone to obey all that Jesus commanded cannot be rushed. It is necessarily patient work.

# TEACHER'S NOTES FOR WEEK 3

## DIGGING IN

1. A missionary's job is to live in another context with the goal of making disciples and starting churches among people or in places where they currently do not exist. Every Christian ought to be involved in evangelism and discipling, but not every Christian will do so in a context that requires as much training (e.g., in language or culture) and sacrifice.

2. Matthew 28:16–20 is the Great Commission delivered; Acts 13–14 is the Great Commission obeyed. It shows us how Paul, in his unique role as an apostle, sought to make disciples of all nations in obedience to the Great Commission.

3. Step 1: Antioch of Syria (13:1–3). Paul and Barnabas are sent off.

Step 2: Seleucia (13:4).

Step 3: Salamis (13:5). They preach with John's help.

Step 4: Paphos (13:6–12). They preach and spar with Bar-Jesus, the false prophet, and Elymas the magician.

Step 5: Perga (13:13). John leaves to go back to Jerusalem.

Step 6: Antioch of Pisidia (13:14–52). Paul and Barnabas preach the gospel to great effect. The Jewish religious leaders didn't like how popular their message was getting, so they began to oppose them. Nonetheless, "as many as were appointed to eternal life believed" (13:48).

Step 7: Iconium (14:1–5). Paul and Barnabas preach again from the synagogue, and again the Jews and Greeks stir up dissension. They remain for "a long time" and only leave when they hear about a plot to stone them.

Step 8: Lystra (14:8–19). Paul miraculously heals a crippled man. The locals mistake Paul and Barnabas for gods; ultimately, the Jews travel to Lystra and stone Paul to the point of near death.

Step 9: Derbe (14:20–21). Paul lives! He and Barnabas preach the gospel in Derbe and make "many disciples" (v. 21).

Steps 10–12: They begin to retrace their steps: Lystra, Iconium, Antioch of Pisidia, and Perga, all places they've been before (except for Attalia; 14:21–25). Why? To strengthen the souls of the disciples, encourage them to continue in the faith, and appoint elders for them in every church.

Step 13: Antioch of Syria (14:26–28). They return to their home church. They gather the church together and declare how God had used them. They stay there "no little time" (v. 28).

4. Paul and Barnabas appoint leaders in every church because they are trying to prepare these regions for faithful ministry long after they're gone. In other words, they're trying to set up healthy churches, which requires the leadership of qualified elders.

5. Clearly, the leading edge of missions *is* evangelism. If you're not sharing the gospel with people who don't believe it, then whatever you're doing is not missions. But notice that Paul and Barnabas's first missionary journey covered a lot more than evangelism and preaching. They were committed to retracing their steps and staying a while. Why? Because they wanted to obey the Great Commission by leaving behind established churches, not simply informal or unorganized groups of Christians.

6–7. Answers will vary.

# TEACHER'S NOTES FOR WEEK 4

## DIGGING IN

1. Answers will vary, but ensure that readers notice how long it takes for Paul and Barnabas to become missionaries who get sent out of the church at Antioch and how these early churches share resources and know one another.

2. They need to be a faithful brother or sister who has already proven themselves disciplined in performing the various tasks of ministry. Their personal sense of calling needs to be confirmed and tested by a local church.

3. It was unique in that the Holy Spirit directly spoke to them (Acts 13:2–3). While churches these days may have a sense of confidence or a gut feeling that the Lord is leading them in a certain direction, they should not expect the kind of verbal confirmation we read about here.

4. Nonetheless, we see a method worth following in Antioch's sending out of Paul and Barnabas—the two apostles have proven themselves to be disciplined in tasks of ministry and have their personal sense of calling confirmed and tested by the church.

5. It communicates that missionaries ought to maintain some kind of accountable relationship with their sending church. This isn't simply a box to be checked. It's an on-ramp to mutual joy, growing fellowship, and glorifying God.

6. Answers will vary.

7. Missions agencies can be helpful by facilitating the relationship between the missionary on the field and the church back home. In other words, they should help bear burdens that most local churches can't bear alone. Often, this includes providing administrative and organizational assistance. Sometimes it includes providing financial support and connecting missionaries to other like-minded folks in their region. Agencies can assist churches in all of this because of their expertise and larger staff. However, missionaries are not only (or primarily) accountable to such agencies; they're primarily accountable to the church (or churches) that sent them out and continue to support their ministry.

# TEACHER'S NOTES FOR WEEK 5

## DIGGING IN

1. Paul has fulfilled his mandate to preach the gospel among the Gentiles from Jerusalem to Illyricum. Yes, many have still not heard the gospel in these areas. But churches have been planted in key centers, and from there Paul's coworkers will bring the gospel to outlying areas (e.g., Epaphras in Colossae; Col. 1:7).[8]

2. To preach the gospel in places where there are no Christians and no churches. In particular, he wants to go to Spain (v. 24).

3. He quotes from Isaiah 52:15, which is from the fourth and final Servant Song. We covered those in some detail in week 1. Here, Paul appeals to this verse to make the point that Christ's death as the suffering servant of the Lord jumpstarts the spread of the gospel to all peoples, just as Isaiah prophesied.

4. We should have the same priorities as Paul, that is, focusing on missions among people groups where there is currently little to no accessible gospel witness. That doesn't mean we should discourage ministry in areas that have already been touched by the gospel but simply that our church's ambitions should mirror Paul's. If your missions budget is weighted toward ministry in places where healthy churches already exist, it's perhaps worth revisiting.

5. He wants their financial support ("to be helped on my journey [to Spain] by you"; Rom. 15:24). But he also wants their company. He doesn't want to be a lone-ranger missionary who uses the church and then leaves it in the dust.

6. He uses these churches as an example of Gentile Christians being generous to Jewish Christians. This precedent of generosity should extend to the Romans too, and he's hopeful they will help him on his way to Spain.

7. He gives the reason for the Gentiles' offering in the next sentence: "For if the Gentiles have come to share in their spiritual blessings, they ought also to be of service to them in material blessings" (15:27). In other words, the Gentiles—which includes his present audience, the Romans—have been

---

[8] Thomas R. Schreiner, study notes for Romans in *ESV Study Bible* (Wheaton, IL: Crossway, 2008), 2183.

adopted into Israel's family. They now enjoy every spiritual blessing as a result of that adoption. Paul's implicit point here is that because spiritual blessings are of far greater value than material blessings, these Gentiles are instinctively happy to contribute to the needs of their brothers and sisters.

8. Answers will vary.

# TEACHER'S NOTES FOR WEEK 6

## DIGGING IN

1. Those who have "gone out for the sake of the name" (v. 7) ought to be supported, that is, sent on "in a manner worthy of God" (v. 6). As we support such people, John says, we become "fellow workers" (v. 8).

2. Generous financial support.

3. Because they've gone out "for the sake of the name" (v. 7) and have not accepted money from non-Christians. (Note: John is using "Gentiles" differently than Paul. John is referring to non-Christians.)

4. They've gone out with the goal of spreading the fame and glory of God through the planting of healthy churches. Those are the kind of missionaries we should support, and we should know those missionaries well enough to be able to say with total confidence that we are "fellow workers for the truth" (v. 8).

5. This letter is a call to love according to the truth. One application of that kind of love is to break off any kind of fellowship with or affirmation of false teachers.

6. The criterion is simple: what they say about Jesus (v. 7). The false teachers in 2 John deny that Jesus came in the flesh. In doing so, they have not "abide[d] in the teaching of Christ" and have shown that they are not born again (v. 9). We should be sure to never endorse any teacher or missionary who makes such egregious errors.

7. We should cut them off and call them out. If we fail to do so, we become guilty of participating in their wicked schemes. According to 3 John, we become "fellow workers" of falsehood (v. 8).

8. At a minimum, a church shouldn't outsource oversight of its missionaries to an agency. It should know who their missionaries are and know what they believe about important doctrinal and ministerial matters. That requires some vetting on the front-end, but it isn't a onetime process. A healthy relationship between a church and a missionary assumes ongoing accountability and fellowship, and ongoing accountability and fellowship requires regular visits. In addition to offering encouragement and support, these visits offer an opportunity to analyze the nature of a

missionary's ministry, which is too difficult to do from halfway around the world.

9. Possible answers include (but are not limited to) unteachability, a refusal to partner with other like-minded believers where they are, a lack of transparency about their work, and a lack of desire for accountability.

# 9Marks

### Building Healthy Churches

9Marks exists to equip church leaders with a biblical vision and practical resources for displaying God's glory to the nations through healthy churches.

To that end, we want to see churches characterized by these nine marks of health:

1. Expositional Preaching
2. Gospel Doctrine
3. A Biblical Understanding of Conversion and Evangelism
4. Biblical Church Membership
5. Biblical Church Discipline
6. A Biblical Concern for Discipleship and Growth
7. Biblical Church Leadership
8. A Biblical Understanding of the Practice of Prayer
9. A Biblical Understanding and Practice of Missions

---

Find all our Crossway titles and other resources at 9Marks.org.

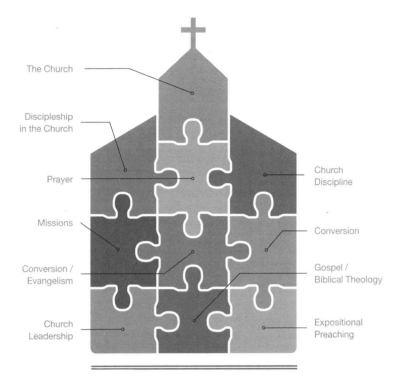

The Church

Discipleship
in the Church

Prayer

Missions

Conversion /
Evangelism

Church
Leadership

Church
Discipline

Conversion

Gospel /
Biblical Theology

Expositional
Preaching

Be sure to check out the rest of the
**9MARKS HEALTHY CHURCH
STUDY GUIDE SERIES**

9Marks Healthy Church Study Guides
is a series of twelve 6–7 week studies
covering the nine distinctives of a
healthy church as laid out in *Nine Marks
of a Healthy Church* by Mark Dever. This
series explores the biblical foundations
of key aspects of the church, helping
Christians live out those realities as
members of a local body.